Contents

Foreword

Gospel music is a vibrant fusion of African folk music and European hymns. Rooted in the spiritual – the creation of African-Americans in the nineteenth century – the spirit and joy of gospel music has gone on to have a profound influence on much twentieth-century pop music. This collection celebrates the path this music has travelled since its inception, from reflective spirituals to uplifting gospel numbers.

The gospel train is a medley of three best-loved gospel songs that would be perfect as a concert opener or encore. Gradually building in momentum, it begins with the laid-back swing of *Go down, Moses* – a traditional spiritual famously used by composer Michael Tippett in his 'Negro Spirituals' – and closes with the unstoppable finale *Ain't no mountain high enough* – a Motown classic that has been recorded by countless artists over the years, including Diana Ross and the Supremes, Marvin Gaye, and the Temptations. The middle song – *Oh happy day!* – was made internationally famous by the Edwin Hawkins Singers in 1969, and then again, for a younger generation, in the film 'Sister Act'. It is now considered one of the best-known gospel standards.

The spiritual *Standing in the need of prayer* is a simple, meditative melody with a pleasing, repetitive chord sequence. This arrangement gives you a chance to 'crank it up a gear' after the modulation; there is also an opportunity to thicken out the vocal harmonies towards the end with some optional alto notes. Once singers get more confident, you may wish to experiment with other improvised harmonies or descants – especially in the last chorus.

Gospel and spirituals grew out of a need to express everyday emotions and to deliver a fundamental message about freedom and hope for a better life. This is not music that should be sung standing still! Encourage your singers to devise simple choreography and/or hand gestures to help deliver the messages of the songs.

Alexander L'Estrange, March 2004

Editorial notes

Choral Basics has been devised to provide arrangements and original pieces specifically for beginner choirs.

Vocal ranges: the arrangements don't explore the extremes of the voice, but aim to stretch the vocal range from time to time in the context of a well-placed musical phrase. Small notes indicate optional alternatives: 1) where the main notes may fall out of comfortable range for some singers, 2) where certain singers on the male-voice part, which mainly falls in the baritone range of a 10th (B–D), wish to explore the tenor or bass register, or 3) where a doubling within a part is suggested.

Breathing: singers should aim to follow the punctuation of the text, and breathe accordingly. However, commas above the music suggest places to breathe where not provided for within the text.

Piano accompaniments: the simple yet imaginative piano parts have been written to support the vocal lines. Small notes in the piano part are intended to help support singers while learning the piece; however, once more confident you may choose to omit the notes, or just to play them very gently.

The gospel train

1. Go down, Moses

arr. Alexander L'Estrange

Traditional Spiritual

8

2. Oh happy day!

words: Philipp Doddridge
music: Edward Francis Rimbault
arr. Edwin R. Hawkins

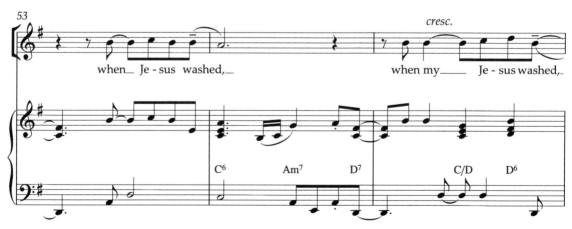

3. Ain't no mountain high enough

words & music: Nicholas Ashford
and Valerie Simpson

Standing in the need of prayer

Traditional Spiritual
arr. Alexander L'Estrange

22

* small notes optional for a few altos